ACKNOWLEDGEMENTS

All the postcards in this book have been selected from the author's collection. The author sincerely acknowledges the help and information given by the following without whom this book would not have been possible:-

Mrs Elan M Rivers, A.L.A., Community Librarian, Llandudno
Mr Huw Tudno Williams, Llandudno
Mr John Nickels, Rhyl
Mr Emrys Jones, Penrhynside, for his kind permission to reproduce the card on page 22
Mr Steve Benz, editing and marketing

LOCAL POSTCARD PUBLISHERS
G.R. Thompson, 15 South Parade. (see page 22)
The ''Chic Studio'' , 43 Mostyn Street
''My Own'' series, Richmond
G.H. Rose, Post Office, Craig-y-Don
R.J. Owens, Clifton Studio, Vaughan Street
H. Jones' series, Lloyd Street
A.E. Vollam, Craig-y-Don, Llandudno and Betws-y-Coed
Slater, Llandudno
John Homan, Arcade, Llandudno
Alec Taylor, West End Post Office, Gloddaeth Street
Bunney's Ltd. (Stationers), Llandudno and Liverpool
W.S. Williams & Sons Ltd., Llandudno
W. Johnson, 159 Mostyn Street & Church Walks, Llandudno
Bamblin, Publishers, 10 Mostyn Street
Evans & Evans, Modern Stationers, St. George's Place
Wilkinson, Photographer, Mostyn Avenue
Fildes Temperance Hotel
J.H. Baxter

LLANDUDNO
"QUEEN OF THE WELSH RESORTS"

Llandudno has retained much of its elegance from its early days when it was planned as a Victorian seaside resort by the Mostyns. Its prosperity grew after 1858 with the coming of the railway and the addition of the pier in the 1870s. The pier enabled visitors to come here for day trips and also to visit other resorts along the North Wales coast. The addition of the Pier Pavilion in the 1880s provided many top entertainers with a venue and an audience in Llandudno.

The history of Llandudno has been well documented over the years. The purpose of this book is to portray the town during a bygone age and to illustrate some of the changes which have occurred over the years.

The photographs are all taken from picture postcards mainly published during the Edwardian era, which is known to collectors as the "Golden Age" of postcards. The history and evolution of the humble postcard has in recent years been published in various books. The most authoritative on this subject is the publication *The Picture Postcard and its Origins* by Frank Staff. Also *Picture Postcards and their Publishers* by Tony Byatt is a valuable source of information on all the major national publishers of postcards.

The only local publisher mentioned in this book is G.R. Thompson of Llandudno, and to quote from Mr Byatt's book, "He occupies an unusual position amongst local publishers because of his claim to be "The Postcard King", and some of his cards carry this name together with his bearded portrait."

Much of the correspondence on the back of these cards is timeless and many of the cards could have been written today. We hope that this book will bring back happy memories for both local people and visitors alike.

Front cover: Great Orme Railway, c. 1905, and the Llandudno coat of arms. The lower shield flanked by two dragons depicts St Tudno's Church. Above the crest is a peer's helm surrounded by an estate mantle. The two shields below depict the arms of the Welsh princes, later the Princes of Wales. The coat of arms is taken from a heraldic postcard published by Stoddard & Co. Ltd of Halifax.

ST TUDNO'S CHURCH, LLANDUDNO.

ST. TUDNO'S CHURCH

No trace of the early 6th-century church survives today. In 1839, the church was seriously damaged during a storm. It was not repaired immediately but in 1855, the church was renovated by W.H. Reece of Birmingham. A new parish church, dedicated to St. George, was built in a more accessible position on the lower slops of the Great Orme in 1840 (see page 5). The postcard is based on a painting by the artist, Elmer Keene.

GLODDAETH HALL, c. 1907

One of the family seats of the Mostyn family who still own much of the land in and around Llandudno. Lady Augusta Mostyn, who died here in 1912, was an important benefactress to the town. She supported many worthy causes and gave financial support for public buildings for the benefit of the townspeople of Llandudno. In 1878 Lady Augusta employed Eden Nesfield to remodel Gloddaeth Hall.

INVALID'S WALK

Invalid's Walk is also known as Lovers' Walk on early maps. In the left background is the Tower House; the Tower in the picture obscured by foliage. This causeway leads to Haulfre Gardens developed by Pochin in the 1870s. He later developed the Bodnant Garden. Haulfre Gardens was opened as a public park by David Lloyd George in 1929.

CHURCH WALKS, c. 1906

A semi-rural scene showing the castellated Bodlondeb on the left and the Royal Hotel on the right.
The Bodlondeb Castle was built as a home by the son of the founder and owner of the St. George's
Hotel, Isaiah Davies, but he never lived there. The Royal Hotel was built as the first major hotel in
Llandudno and was originally known as the Mostyn Arms.

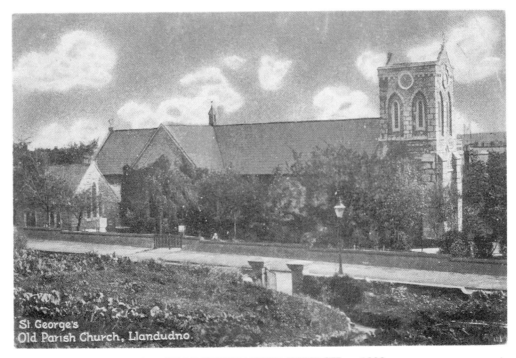

ST. GEORGE'S PARISH CHURCH, c. 1908

St. George's Church in Church Walks situated on the lower slops of the Great Orme, was built in 1840 by John Welch. The church replaced St. Tudno's Church which had been seriously damaged in a storm. A number of interesting graves lie in the churchyard. The old-style gas lamps have nearly all disappeared from the town today.

5

North Madoc Street, Llandudno.

NORTH MADOC STREET

North Madoc Street was later renamed Arvon Avenue. The spire of Christ Church is seen peeping
above the hotels in the right background.

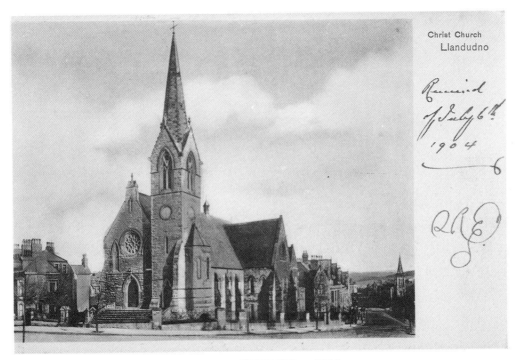

Christ Church
Llandudno

Received
of July 6th
1904

CHRIST CHURCH, c. 1905

Christ Church was built in 1857 with the tower added at a later date. Sadly, part of the spire was demolished as it was thought to be unsafe. Christ Church stands at the top of Arvon Avenue, previously known as North Madoc Street. There are a number of churches and chapels in Llandudno that were built in response to the demand for English services by both visitors and new residents.

LLEWELYN AVENUE, c. 1911

A turn of the century view of the present Llewelyn Avenue, showing on the left the well-established business of the grocer, Mr. Roberts of Roby House. Across the road is the Welsh Baptist Chapel, Tabernacle, shown here in its rebuilt classical style of 1876.

Empire Hotel, Upper Mostyn Street, Llandudno.

THE EMPIRE HOTEL, UPPER MOSTYN STREET, c. 1905

The Empire Hotel started its early days as an Italian warehouse under the ownership of Thomas Williams who also wrote an early guide book to the town. On the right of the picture is Gadlys House and Hendre House. The block of boarding houses continues to descend the hill to Mostyn Street. Some of these properties were built by Carters of London during the early 1860s.

UPPER MOSTYN STREET, c. 1910

On the left of the picture is T. Esmor Hooson's shop, still owned by the Hooson family and one of the oldest Llandudno families still trading in 1991. On the near right of the picture is the Post Office which has moved its premises a number of times in order to be near the centre of activities in the town. The first post office in Llandudno was opened in October 1838, at 'Greenhill', 18 Old Road.

Mostyn Street, and Great Orme, Llandudno.

MOSTYN STREET, c. 1911

A single-deck car of the Llandudno and Colwyn Bay Electric Railway passes the ''clock'' in the left foreground. The ''clock'' which is still there today was given for the benefit of the residents of Llandudno by Richard Owen in 1875. The Llandudno and C.B.E.R. came to Llandudno in 1907. In the right foreground, next to the Cambridge Restaurant, is Trehearne's, bookseller, stationer, library, who also sold picture postcards.

MOSTYN STREET, c. 1920

Arthur's Pioneer Stores, as seen in the postcard, burnt down in 1923. It was rebuilt and then burnt down again. It was opened by the Williams family of Marie et Cie, who also owned other "Pioneer" stores in the town. After the second fire Clare's Department Store eventually bought the site and they are still trading today. On the left is the Picture House which started its life as the St. George's Hall: the site is now occupied by the "Lo Cost" grocery store.

MOSTYN STREET, c. 1932

The shopping centre in the thirties. Gone are the landaus and horse-drawn carriages — replaced by motor cars and trams. Fondly remembered stores such as Star Supplies, Maypole and Arnold's, shown on the right have now sadly disappeared.

MOSTYN STREET, 1900s

Prior to mechanisation and the advent of the trams in 1907, the horse carriages had stands in Upper Mostyn Street and Gloddaeth Avenue where the taxi stands are now sited.

MOSTYN STREET, p.u. 1906

On the left is Samuel Bartley's drapery store situated at Compton House and Yeovil House. The properties were later demolished and replaced by the National Provincial Bank (now National Westminster) in the 1920s when they moved from their previous location at Wilton House, Prince Edward Square.

BUNNEY'S CORNER, MOSTYN STREET, p.u. 1905

Bunney's was one of the most popular stores in the town for both locals and visitors. (Published by Bunney's of Liverpool and Llandudno).

Mostyn Street, Llandudno. 15751.

THE SAVOY CINEMA, MOSTYN STREET

The popular Savoy Cinema was built as the Picture House in 1914 and closed in 1988. It was the first cinematograph building in Llandudno and had two serious fires, one in 1942 and the other in 1957. Notice the iron verandah.

L 396   MOSTYN STREET, LLANDUDNO

MOSTYN STREET, early 1920s

In the right foreground is the Oriental Stores — still in business today. On the left is Bamblin's and their umbrella repair business, and also shown is Brookes's — an old Llandudno family business.

Mostyn Street, Llandudno.

MOSTYN STREET AND THE NORTH WESTERN GARDENS, 1900s

Originally, the Gardens were for the use of the North Western Hotel residents. Public toilets were built underground in the 1920s. On the left of the picture is a busy scene by County Auction Mart above which are the words Post Card Palace. No doubt they are buying postcards!

NORTH WESTERN HOTEL AND NEW GARDENS, LLANDUDNO.

THE NORTH WESTERN HOTEL, c. 1925

Originally two hotels, The Tudno and the Temperance, the North Western Hotel took its name from the old railway company. The gardens belonged to the Hotel, but were taken over by the Llandudno U.D.C. When the Prince of Wales visited the town in November 1923, a floral arch was erected between the North Western and Red Garages to welcome the Royal party. A similar arch was erected over the road at the Craig-y-Don promenade end urging the Prince to "hurry back".

GLODDOETH STREET, LLANDUDNO.

HOOSON'S CORNER, GLODDAETH STREET, c. 1910

J. Esmor Hooson came to Llandudno in 1870 from a mining background. Hooson's shop has been on this corner for well over a hundred years. The low building near The Clarence Hotel is Thomas Edge's photographic studio. In the middle distance is Seilo Chapel; rebuilt in 1905.

G.R. THOMPSON

G.R. Thompson was a local postcard publisher who claimed to be ''The Postcard King'' probably because of his resemblance to King Edward VII as most of his cards bear his bearded portrait, and one of the main retailers of local postcards in the town. This postcard shows one of his shops at 15 South Parade. His other premises were at 63a Mostyn Street (now the popular coffee centre), 18 Mostyn Street, 15 Gloddaeth Street, a stall on Llandudno Pier and also a shop at Deganwy. Mr Thompson died in 1929 and his grandson, Mr Smith, ran the business, G.R. Thompson & Sons Ltd., until its closure in September 1985.

GLODDAETH STREET, c. 1930s

On the left, next to E.B. Jones, grocer, is A.E. Vollam's post office and postcard shop. Vollam's started business in Craig-y-Don in 1895 and moved to Gloddaeth Street in the early 1920s, where they started to produce their own postcards. The Palladium Cinema, shown in the centre, was built in 1920 on the site of an old market hall. Also shown in the right background, beyond the church, is the Astra Cinema, built in 1934 on the site of a former garage and now demolished.

RISBORO' BOARDING HOUSE, 1, CLEMENT AVENUE, LLANDUDNO.

RISBORO' BOARDING HOUSE, 1 CLEMENT AVENUE

The Risboro' was erected as W.A. Whistons' Collegiate Boys School in 1887. Later in 1896, it became the first John Bright School; initially for boys only. Today it is one of Llandudno's finest hotels.

24

ONE ASH, GLODDAETH AVENUE, LLANDUDNO.

ONE ASH, GLODDAETH AVENUE,

An interesting postcard advertising the One Ash Hotel where the writer of this postcard was staying in 1910. Presumably, this hotel was called the One Ash after the home of the Rochdale M.P., John Bright who spent many holidays in Llandudno. In the middle distance is the cupola (tower) of Seilo Chapel rebuilt on this site in 1905. In the far distance is a pleasure-steamer about to dock at the pier.

CHAPEL STREET, LLANDUDNO.

CHAPEL STREET, c. 1912

Ebeneser Chapel is situated on the corner of Lloyd and Chapel Streets. The present circular domed chapel was rebuilt on this site in 1909 by the architect, W. Beddoe Rees. The pews in this chapel were considered outstanding by Anthony Jones, author of a book on Welsh chapels.

CHAPEL STREET, c. 1905

Showing the more relaxed nature of life in the days of the horse and cart. Nowadays, this street is almost always packed with cars often double-parked. The loss of the trees is also notable. Presumably the street was named after the Ebeneser Chapel to the rear of the photographer and recently converted into a privately-run community hall by Mr & Mrs Frank Gorka. On the left can be seen the spire of the English Presbyterian Church which replaced a corrugated-iron structure built on this site in 1880. The present building replaced an earlier structure in 1891.

27

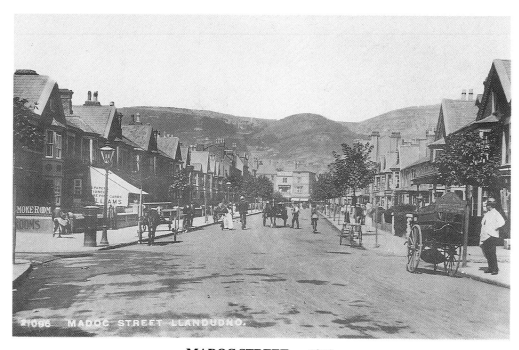

MADOC STREET, c. 1912

This street of two-storey houses was built in the 1870s to accommodate the people of Llandudno who were displaced from their homes along the seashore following the enforcement of the Enclosure Acts and the allocation of land to existing landowners. Some of the houses had stables and shippons at the rear. Many of these houses have now been converted to shops.

DRUMMOND VILLA, TRINITY SQUARE, LLANDUDNO.
1 minute from Sea, 3 minutes from Station, 5 minutes from Pier.

TRINITY SQUARE, c. 1906

Drummond Villa has been a boarding establishment for most of its years and was run by a G. Webb in 1892, then unsuccessfully short-listed to be the first John Bright Secondary School in 1896. It is currently occupied by the regional headquarters of the National Trust.

LLANDUDNO. The Railway Station.

THE RAILWAY STATION, c. 1905

Evocative of the days when most visitors to Llandudno arrived by train. The railway came to
Llandudno in 1858. The present railway station was built in 1891 in response to the increasing
number of visitors to the town.

AUGUSTA STREET, c. 1912

Griffith's Temperance Hotel is shown on the left and the railway station is shown in the right background. The stables of the Llandudno Coaching and Carriage Co. can be seen in the middle distance; these stables later housed the coaches of the Royal Blues and until recently they housed Crosville buses.

AUGUSTA STREET, c. 1913

Looking in the opposite direction to page 31. Showing on the left, the horses and carts waiting outside the railway station, ready to convey passengers luggage — the passengers following in more roomy carriages. The low building on the left carrying an advertisement for the Egyptian Hall was a dairy and sweet shop. The Egyptian Hall was originally part of the Pier Pavilion complex.

Fildes' "Welcome" Hotel (with sea view.)

Vaughan Street, Llandudno, C.27.

VAUGHAN STREET, c. 1912

This terrace of boarding houses and shops in Vaughan Street were designed by the architect, Mr G.A. Humphreys who was also the agent to the Mostyn Estate. In the far distance at the end of the terrace can be seen the Mostyn Art Gallery. The Post Office was built in 1904.

COLWYN ROAD, CRAIGSIDE

A nostalgic view of the eastern side of Llandudno when one could stroll leisurely and safely.
Today, Colwyn Road, Craigside, is one of the main traffic routes into and out of the resort.

Handwritten on postcard: Roman Coins und on the Little Orme's Head, January 10th 1907. and Emperor Carausius A.D. 293.

Ye Olde Curiosity Shoppe, 20, BACK MOSTYN STREET

HOLLAND'S CHINA ROOM
Westminster Buildings, Lloyd Street, Llandudno.

Photo by SLATER, LLANDUDNO.

DISCOVERY OF ROMAN COINS, 10.1.1907

An unusual postcard showing part of a hoard of Roman coins unearthed in a bank about 12 yards from the highway at Craigside, opposite the stable entrance to Shimdda Hir, now Craigside Manor. They were carted down and dumped between St. Paul's Church and the Grand Theatre during the construction of the Mostyn Broadway. The discovery came to light the following morning.

VIEW FROM THE LITTLE ORME, c. 1905

Llandudno from the Little Orme, showing in the left foreground the Craigside Hydro Hotel built in 1888. Its laundry provided many jobs for women who lived in the area as did the Little Orme quarry for the men. In March 1951, H.R.H. Princess Margaret visited the hotel for lunch.

NANT GAMAR Rᴰ LLANDUDNO. 407-88

NANT-Y-GAMAR ROAD

Some of the oldest property in Craig-y-Don can be found on Nant-y-Gamar Road including Bethania Chapel, which is just obscured by the trees on the right of the postcard. Craig-y-Don did not develop until after 1884. Before this date the land formed part of the Peers Williams estate which included Penrhyn Old Hall. Craig-y-Don was named after the Williams' Craig-y-Don Estate on Anglesey.

CD 9   MOSTYN AVENUE. LOOKING NORTH, CRAIG-Y-DON   A 'TUCK CARD

MOSTYN AVENUE

Dunphy's corner at the junction of Queen's Road and Mostyn Avenue, Craig-y-Don. The Dunphys originally came from Ireland and their business expanded fast. They had shops in Mostyn Street, Craig-y-Don, Deganwy, and a warehouse opposite the old fire station in Market Street, Llandudno. In emergencies they occasionally lent their horses to the Llandudno Fire Brigade. The church on the far right is the Duke of Clarence Church, St. Paul's.

Queens Road, Llandudno

QUEEN'S ROAD, c. 1914

Queen's Road, Craig-y-Don, was named after Queen Victoria. This area of Llandudno has developed as mostly freehold properties. It was not owned by the Mostyns and so developed on a different scale to the rest of the planned Victorian resort. Many of the streets were named after the Queen Elisabeth of Roumania (Carmen Sylva), because of her visit and stay in the town during 1890.

BRYN HOTEL AND TENNIS COURTS, QUEENS ROAD

Craig-y-Don traditionally had first-class tennis facilities. Llandudno's first Lawn Tennis Tournament was held at Messrs Riddell and Jarvis' newly erected lawn tennis ground on August 5th and 6th, 1885 on the site of St. David's English Methodist Church. The men's singles winner was Mr Goodacre, and Mrs Pickering won the ladies title. Local solicitor, Mr J. C. Parke played in both singles and doubles in 1912 when Britain won the Davis Cup.

CARMEN SYLVA ROAD FROM PROMENADE, CRAIG-Y-DON, LLANDUDNO. W.117.

CARMEN SYLVA ROAD

Carmen Sylva Road was named after ''Carmen Sylva'', the pen name for the Queen of Roumania who stayed in Llandudno in 1890. She was an authoress and came to Llandudno to recuperate from an illness.

PENRHYNSIDE

PENRHYNSIDE VILLAGE, c. 1900

Many of the villagers worked in the quarries on the Little Orme; the first quarry founded in 1889
by a Lancashire man. During the first world war many women carried out many manual duties
such as loading, blasting, driving the trains and loading the ships.

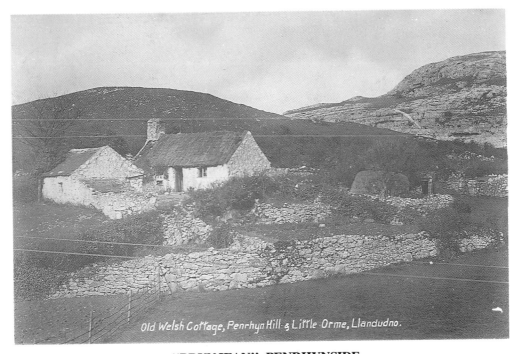

Old Welsh Cottage, Penrhyn Hill & Little Orme, Llandudno.

"BRYN IFAN", PENRHYNSIDE

One of the last thatched properties in the Llandudno area. This cottage featured along with a neighbouring cottage "Siop y Roe" on picture postcards at the beginning of this century with ladies dressed in Welsh costume.

Penrhyn Hall
1907.

·DG.M·I·

A Mediaeval Manor House (A.D. 1422), once the residence of Archbishop Williams of York, keeper of the Great Seal of James I. Containing fifteen rooms equipped with a remarkable collection of Old Welsh Oak, Relics, and Curios—Admission 6d. Hill Tea Gardens, profuse with old-world flowers, for high-class 1/- Teas—attendants in Welsh Costumes. Henry VI. period chapel free to visitors—in garden adjoining.

PENRHYN OLD HALL

Penrhyn Old Hall, Penrhyn Bay, was the home of Robert Pugh, a staunch Roman Catholic, who fled with a small group of refugees to a cave on the Little Orme Head in 1586, during the Protestant religious persecution in the reign of Elizabeth I. The Catholics set up an illegal press and, in the most difficult conditions, produced a small booklet titled Y Drych Cristionogol (The Christian Mirror) for secret circulation. The cave was eventually discovered in April 1587 but everyone managed to escape. The remains of the Pughs of Penrhyn's private chapel can still be seen on the north-east end of the main house. The house is now occupied by a night club.

GENERAL VIEW WEST SHORE, LLANDUDNO

WEST SHORE

West Shore in its infancy, showing the remains of the old jetty. The yacht pool was constructed in 1896, and supplied water from the mountain springs which flowed through the old mine workings. In the foreground is Glan-y-Don cottage. The only ship built in Llandudno, the *Sarah Lloyd*, was constructed at the bottom of the garden of Glan-y-Don cottage in 1863.

GOGARTH ABBEY HOTEL, c. 1907

Part of this hotel was built in 1862 as Penmorfa, the holiday home of Dean Liddell. The author, Lewis Carroll may have visited the Liddell's at Penmorfa, and it is said that his book *Alice in Wonderland* was written here. The main character, Alice, modelled on Alice, the Liddell's daughter.

THE MARINE DRIVE, c. 1911

The Marine Drive was constructed between 1875-88 and replaced the original hazardous path. During a visit to Llandudno in 1868, Prime Minister Gladstone had to be blind-folded, seated on a mule, when negotiating the old route. The views from Marine Drive are incomparable and breathtaking, and the distance around from gate to gate is just over four miles.

Nose of the Great Orme, Llandudno.

Lighthouse, Llandudno.

THE LIGHTHOUSE, GREAT ORMES HEAD

Before the lighthouse was built, no local navigational marks existed in spite of the busy sea traffic to and from the Dee and Mersey ports. The Mersey Docks and Harbour Board eventually established and built the castellated lighthouse in 1862, maintaining it until 1973 when it was handed over to Trinity House. The light, which was visible for 21 miles, was housed in a 37 ft-high tower built in front of the fortress-like building and situated on the cliff edge 325 feet above high water level. The lighthouse is no longer owned by Trinity House and is now privately owned. The original light is now part of an exhibition on show at the summit of the Great Orme.

LLETTY'R FILIAST

A megalithic chamber tomb known as Lletty'r Filiast. It can be seen today in a field off Cromlech Road, Great Orme.

Dolmen (commonly called "Cromlech"), on Gt. Orme's Head, Llandudno

"Dolmen," of which the literal meaning is "stone table," from "daul" (table) and "maen" (stone), is a *stone burial chamber*, roughly resembling a table in form, originally covered over with earth, forming a mound known as a "barrow." The inhabitants of Britain in prehistoric times —i.e., at a date anterior to the Christian Era—made use of such structures for the interment of their dead. The name "Cromlech" has been frequently used by Welsh archæologists for such stone structures.—*G.A.H., Llandudno, 1908.*

Copper Mines, Maes-y-Facrell. Gt. Orme's Head.   Llandudno.

COPPER MINES, MAES-Y-FACRELL, c. 1903

The wall-covered ''Vivian's shaft'', which extended over 500 ft. to below sea level, was the hub of Great Orme mining during the 18th and 19th centuries and had been mined since prehistoric times. This area was opened as a tourist attraction on 23rd April 1991.

The Old Farm on Great Orme, the nearest way to the summit, and St. Tudno's Church, Llandudno.

Septer 6th 1906

WHITE FARM, c. 1906

Penmynydd Isa, now known as White Farm. A typical Celtic-style single-storey house dating back to a time when Llandudno depended on farming and copper mining for its prosperity.

BRITISH AND BRITISH EMPIRE
LIGHT-HEAVYWEIGHT CHAMPION

SOUVENIR from RANDY S BAR
and Holiday Centre Great Orme, Llandudno.

RANDOLPH TURPIN

Randolph Turpin (1928-1966) was world middleweight boxer in 1951. He bought the Summit Hotel shortly afterwards and made it into a tourist attraction with a boxing exhibition and other family entertainments. He took part in boxing bouts from time to time in the ring outside the hotel. He ran into financial problems and the hotel was sold to the council in 1961. He died at his home in Leamington, Warwickshire in 1966.

Great Orme Holiday Centre, Llandudno.

THE SUMMIT HOTEL

The Summit Hotel originally the Great Orme Hotel, was the idea of a Mr Morgan, the owner of the Clarence Hotel. This hotel was built on the site of the former Telegraph Station which was part of a Victorian semaphore system between Holyhead and Liverpool. The Summit Hotel was owned by the world middleweight boxer Randolph Turpin from 1952-1961. At one time the hotel included a very popular 18-hole golf course.

GREAT ORME HOTEL AND GREAT ORME RAILWAY, LLANDUDNO

THE GREAT ORME RAILWAY

The Great Orme Railway is unique in Britain in that its construction is a remote control funicular line. The railway was authorised by an Act of Parliament in 1898, with its construction, which commenced in April 1901, and completed in 1903, divided into two sections, lower and upper, with a guage of 3ft 6ins. The lower section, opened on 1st July 1902, is 872 yards long with its steepest gradient 1:3.9. The upper section, opened on 8th July 1903, is 827 yards long with its steepest gradient 1:10.3. The two cars on each section (numbers 4 and 5 on the lower, and numbers 6 and 7 on the upper) are fixed to the winding rope, the winding drum converted from steam to electricity in 1958. The overhead wire serves for telephone and bell communication. The four cars were built by Hurst Nelson of Motherwell; 4 and 5 in 1902 and 6 and 7 in 1903. The railway has had three owners; the original company went into liquidation in 1933 (following a fatal accident in 1932), and the line was taken over by the Llandudno U.D.C. in 1949.

54

FACING THE SEA
AND
GRAND PROMENADE

| Telegrams | { St. George's Hotel, Llandudno. | **ST. GEORGE'S HOTEL, LLANDUDNO.** | Telephone | { Proprietor, No. 7. Visitors, No. 300. |

ST. GEORGE'S HOTEL

The original building was opened in 1854 as the Isaiah Davies family hotel and further additions were made in 1878 to the designs of George Felton, the Mostyn agent. The hotel remained in the ownership of the descendants of the Davies', who built the original hotel, until the 1970s.

ST. GEORGE AND PRINCE OF WALES HOTELS

St. George's Hotel is reputed to be the first hotel to be built on the promenade. The Prince of Wales Hotel is now entirely turned over to retail premises but was at one time an antique room run by Frederick Holland of 91, Mostyn Street. He was a collector of local artifacts which included the locally famous Roman coin hoard discovered on the Little Orme (see page 34).

Hydro, Neville Crescent, *Llandudno.*

Thanks for letter —

THE HYDRO, NEVILLE CRESCENT

Dr Thomas opened the Neville Hydro in 1860 offering hydropathic treatment. Today the hotel is still busy and part of the large Pleasurama Group which includes Shearings Coach and Bus Company. The hotel deals solely with coach groups at present.

THE WASHINGTON HOTEL

In 1854, the original site was occupied by two houses called "Fair View" standing in isolation. The buildings were converted into the Little Ormes Head Hotel in 1865, but renamed the Washington Hotel in 1870. As the building protruded dangerously about 50 feet out from its present site, it was decided to demolish the hotel. The present Washington Hotel was completed in 1925.

Craig-Y-Don Promenade, Llandudno

CRAIG-Y-DON c. 1912

Looking along the Promenade and showing the original site of the Washington Hotel (see page 57), and how it protruded out of line with the other terraced hotels. Notice the portable bandstand on the promenade which used to be regularly transported to other locations on the sea-front walk.

The Craig-y-don Boarding Establishment, Llandudno

THE COUNTY HOTEL

The Craig-y-Don was renamed the County, and for many years was run by the snooker champion, Fred Davies. His more famous brother, Joe, then rated the world's best player, drew large audiences when playing exhibition matches with Fred.

LLANDUDNC

—

ORMESCLIFF

PRIVATE

HOTEL.

CHARABANC TOUR, ORMESCLIFFE HOTEL

Five charabancs hired for the residents of the Ormescliffe Private Hotel, lined up and ready to depart for a tour of the locality. Notice the solid rubber-tyred wheels, the fold-down hoods, and the short bonnets which concealed a long-stroke engine.

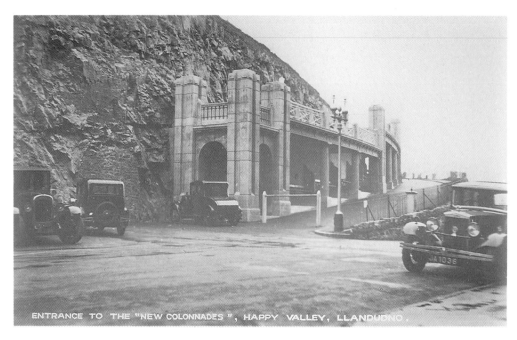

ENTRANCE TO THE "NEW COLONNADES", HAPPY VALLEY, LLANDUDNO.

THE COLONNADE

The Colonnade was opened in 1932 and proved popular with both visitors and locals as a route to the Happy Valley. The bricked-up entrance, noticeable on the cliff wall, enclosed an old wine cellar which serviced the Baths Hotel; the hotel was demolished in 1900.

Happy Valley,
(presented to the Town as a Jubilee gift
in 1887 by Lord Mostyn)
and Gt. Orme, Llandudno.

HAPPY VALLEY

The Happy Valley was another donation to the town by the Mostyn family. For many years the site in the foreground was occupied by an open-air theatre and was a popular venue. The middle distance now has many mature trees which presumably were planted at around this time. A small statue to Queen Victoria appears in the middle right of the picture, though the bust was stolen and later recovered and is now in the care of the local authority.

LLANDUDNO TOWN BAND, c. 1950

The band used to entertain in the Happy Valley Amphitheatre for many years on Sunday afternoons. Following the retirement of Mr. Traversi in 1948, Mr. Bill Skelton, a Lancastrian (inset), took over as conductor until 1952.

HAPPY VALLEY

J. Codman's Entertainers were part of a long tradition of entertainment which started in the Happy Valley in 1873. The Happy Valley remained popular entertainment for the visitors right through to the 1950s and 1960s, with Waldini and his band, and latterly that intrepid Scotsman, Alex Monro.

C. H. WILKINSON   1936 HAPPY VALLEY REVELS   CRAIG-Y-DON
LLANDUDNO

HAPPY VALLEY

Dance troupes and pierrots became very popular in the 1920s and 1930s. Many famous troupes appeared in Llandudno including the Fol de Rols, Adeler and Sutton's Pierrots and of course the most famous of all, Will Catlin and his Royal Pierrots.

HAPPY VALLEY, c. 1914

Churchill's Minstrels at Happy Valley. Billy Churchill had the honour of appearing before the King and Queen in the first Royal Command Performance at the Palace Theatre on 1st July, 1912.

The late Messrs Joe Parry and Alf Allan, in the Court Scene, Happy Valley, Llandudno 1902.

HAPPY VALLEY

Joe Perry (not Parry as printed on card) is shown with Alf Allan performing from their little white tents in the Happy Valley. Clarkson Rose, a well-known entertainer who remembers their act well, said ''out of the tents came Perry and Allan's minstrels with fat Mr. Perry in control and the mournful Joe Allan, perched on his chair waiting to sing 'sucking cider through a straw'...'' They also performed in the New Princes Theatre, and on the promenade.

PERFORMING BIRDS

For many years, the Victorian entertainer, Mr. Giciano Ferrari thrilled audiences on the promenade with his superbly trained birds who performed incredible tricks. Born in Italy, he came to Llandudno from Brighton, and had a shop and home in Somerset Street. He died in 1923. His gravestone in Llanrhos churchyard is embellished with doves.

THE CODMAN FAMILY'S PUNCH AND JUDY SHOW c. 1906

The Punch and Judy show has been performing in Llandudno since the 1860s. In the early days, the performance was given on the site of the Clarence Hotel.

THE MAY QUEEN

The choosing of the May Queen in Llandudno commenced in 1892 and continued right through to the 1950s with the exception of three years during the second world war. The May Queen was usually crowned in the Happy Valley but the Pier Pavilion was used when the weather was wet.

MAY DAY PARADE

The tradesman in the picture may have been taking part in one of Llandudno's May Day Parades. There were many different classes in the trades' section including single horse-decorated turnouts and pairs decorated turnouts. The May Day Parades in Llandudno started in 1892 and continued until the early 1950s.

1st PRIZE
Thomas Williams
Remover & Upholsterer
John St Llandudno

MAY DAY PARADE

Thomas Williams appears to have won first prize with his tradesmen's turnout for the May Day parade. There were various categories in these parades for heavy turnouts, light trade vehicles and in this picture the staff appear to be very proud of their achievements.

THE BEACH

A beach scene, showing the Pier Pavilion, built in the 1880s, and, to the right of the picture, the Baths Hotel built in 1855 as a Reading Room and Billiards Room. Later pictures of this scene show the Grand Hotel, built 1901, on the site of the Baths Hotel shown on this postcard. The beach was divided up into separate areas for bathing for women and men until 1894 when mixed bathing was allowed. Notice the bathing-machines on the right.

LLANDUDNO'S DONKEY BOY AND HIS FAVOURITES.

THE DONKEYS

A familiar sight on the beach was the donkeys, who have been giving pleasure to young and old for over a century. The Hughes family, who originate from Llandudno, introduced the donkeys to the town and are still carrying on the business. Notice the Llandudno coat of arms embossed on the postcard.

Camera-Hill and Pavilion from Gloddaeth Street, Llandudno.

THE PROMENADE

The Grand Hotel, Pier Pavilion and Camera Obscura are shown in this picture. Many famous stars have appeared at the Pier Pavilion over the years including Paul Robeson, Semprini, Petula Clark, Cliff Richard and the Beatles. The Camera Obscura was built above the Happy Valley amphitheatre in 1860 and was burnt down in 1966. A replacement has appeared in the last couple of years.

PIER ENTRANCE, LLANDUDNO

PIER ENTRANCE

A view of Prince Edward Square from the Pier. The advertisement above the entrance is for the
evening concerts given every Sunday in the Pier Pavilion at 8.15 p.m. The children's boating area
in the foreground has now been replaced by the Golden Goose Amusements Arcade.

THE PIER

The Pier was opened in 1877 with its main entrance from the promenade being added in 1884. Orchestral concerts were held at the Pier Head from the beginning, and this was where most of John Morava's work with a more popular style of orchestra started in 1938. Some of the main concerts were held in the Pier Pavilion, but during the second world war a temporary bandstand known as the "cowshed" was erected half way along the Pier. The Pier-end Pavilion was used for furniture storage for the Grand Hotel during this period.

THE PIER PAVILION

Residents and visitors strolling along outside the Pier Pavilion (built 1886) in the early part of this century. The Pier Pavilion Orchestra under the conductorship of Jules Riviere played at the Pier Pavilion until 1891 when Riviere fell out with the directors and started his own Riviere's Concert Hall (now the Arcadia). The young Henry Wood first encountered Riviere at this hall and described his first glimpse of the famous conductor in a most unflattering way. The Pier Pavilion changed over to variety shows just before the second world war.

PANORAMA

Llandudno from Green Hill showing very little development in Craig-y-Don. The Links Hotel, in the centre, stands in isolation prior to the building of the Council estates. Conwy Road was built in 1844 as one of the main routes into the then hamlet.

LAUNCH OF THE LIFEBOAT

Showing the launch of the lifeboat *Sunlight No. 1* (1887- 1902) or the *Theodore Price* (1902-1930).
The first Llandudno lifeboat was named *The Sisters' Memorial* and was launched in 1861.

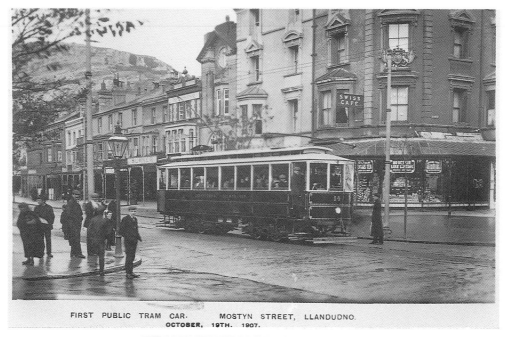

FIRST PUBLIC TRAM CAR.   MOSTYN STREET, LLANDUDNO.
OCTOBER, 19TH. 1907.

THE FIRST PUBLIC TRAM CAR, 1907

Until the electric tramway started service in October 1907 communication between Llandudno and Colwyn Bay was either by horse-bus or steam railway with the inconvenience of a change at Llandudno Junction Station. The trams, originally 14 in number, quickly became popular and a further 4 were ordered with specially deep opening windows to let in the sea breezes in the summer. Similar trams still exist in Portugal even today. Further open-top trams were ordered just before the first world war but were not delivered until 1920. These were the famous 'toastracks'.

    The tramway was abandoned in March 1956 and all but one of the cars dismantled.

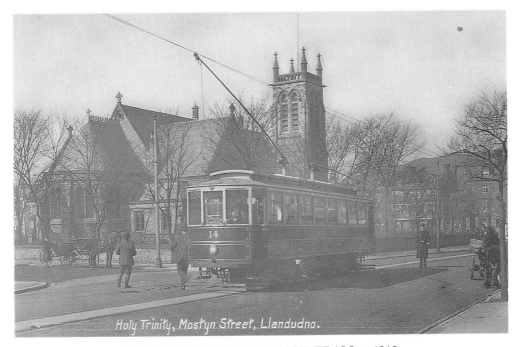

Holy Trinity, Mostyn Street, Llandudno.

HOLY TRINITY CHURCH AND TRAM, c. 1910

In the background stands Holy Trinity Church on land given to the church by the Mostyn family. The foundation stone was laid in 1865, not by Lady Augusta Mostyn as inscribed, but by Mrs K A Morgan, wife of the rector. The church was consecrated and used for worship in 1874. The tram is the last of a batch of 14 used to open the line as far as Rhos-on-Sea, later extended to Colwyn Bay and Old Colwyn. This early view demonstrates the early single track nature of the line which was extensively doubled in the mid-late 1920s. Much of the line was off the highway passing through Bodafon Fields; its course still visible today.

PENRHYN HILL CUTTING, c. 1908

The Llandudno and Colwyn Bay Electric Railway Company opened their service as far as Rhos-on-Sea in October 1907. The track was originally a single line with loops for tram-cars to pass each other. The tramway encouraged the selling of housing plots, particularly in Penrhyn Bay and Rhos-on-Sea. Traffic grew and within a few years the line became a double track. The photograph shows one of the original tram-cars, number two, climbing Penrhyn Hill to Bryn-y-Bia Road. The annual number of passengers carried on the trams eventually reached an amazing record of 2.7 million persons.

THE SILVER MOTOR BUS COMPANY

Showing an early 'bus of the Silver Motor Bus Service, possibly outside Conwy Castle. The "Silvers" or North Wales Silver Company had a garage on Mostyn Broadway which was later taken over by Crosville. It is now a car garage and petrol station. The Silver Motor Bus Services ran their 'buses around the area even as far as Abergele during the 1920s.

SILVER MOTOR BUS CHARABANCS

An outing in charabancs belonging to the Silver Motor Bus Co. Their ''armchair'' charabancs comfortably seated four passengers abreast rather than the usual five. The Royal Blue Coach company who also operated a similar service, called their charabancs ''easy-chair style''. This photograph was taken outside Deganwy Railway Station.

HORSE-DRAWN COACH EXCURSION, c. 1904

Wheeler's Coach Tours could be booked at such places as G.R. Thompson's newsagents. The North Western Hotel started out as two hotels but by 1892 it was called the Tudno Castle. It was known as the North Western Hotel for many years, but reverted back to its earlier name, the Tudno Castle Hotel. The hotel is now known as the Castle.

CHARABANC OUTING

This real photographic postcard, showing a charabanc outing of the Shop Assistants Union, was taken by the 'Chic' Studio, 43 Mostyn Street, Llandudno. The full wording on the board in front of the charabanc is ''National Amalgamated Union of Shop Assistants Warehousemen and Clerks'' followed by ''To obtain the greatest advantages under the National Insurance Act all shop workers should insure with the above Society''.

"LA MARGUERITE", c. 1912

The *La Marguerite* paddle-steamer was described as the largest excursion steamer of her time. She commenced sailings in the 1904 season from Liverpool, calling each day at Llandudno, Beaumaris, Bangor and Menai Bridge. She was broken up in 1925 after being used in the first world war as a troop carrier. (See also *Liverpool to North Wales pleasure-steamers* by John Cowell, published in the same series).

P.S. "ST TUDNO", c. 1910

This is the second *St Tudno* but the first paddle-steamer to be built for the Liverpool and North Wales Steamship Co. in 1891. She was sold in 1912 and broken up 10 years later.

New Town Hall, Llandudno

Valentine's Series

THE TOWN HALL

The splendid Town Hall was built in 1902 by a local builder, R. Luther Roberts, and designed by T.B. Silcock. Part of the site was previously a builder and coal merchant's yard owned by the Hughes family who themselves built property in Llandudno. The previous Town Hall was "Capri" on Church Walks.

New Post Office, Llandudno.

THE "NEW" POST OFFICE,
c. 1904

The Post Office building in Vaughan Street was built, on the site of the 1894 National Eisteddfod, by Mr. Owen Thomas, father of the then Chairman of the Council, who was in his 81st year. He was the oldest builder in the town and he had also built the first house in Llandudno. The Post Office was opened on 20th May 1904 by Lord Stanley, the Postmaster General. The size of the building shows the increased importance of postal services to the growing seaside resort of Llandudno.

LLANDUDNO POST OFFICE STAFF

In later years, the upper floors of the new post office building were altered to accommodate the Llandudno Telephone Exchange and Telegraph Office, where most of the ladies were employed. On the photograph, notice the row of post office delivery boys in the foreground.

LLANRHOS TEMPERANCE HOTEL, LLANDUDNO.

LLANRHOS TEMPERANCE HOTEL, c. 1908

Llanrhos Temperance Hotel was built under the direction of Lady Augusta Mostyn as a cocoa house. Part of the premises was later used as a sub-post office for Llanrhos. At the end of the 19th century, there were two public houses in Llanrhos. Due to their close proximity to Llanrhos Church, it was decided by Lady Mostyn that they should both be demolished. The Mostyn Arms public house was rebuilt in 1898 on a new site further down Conwy Road, nearer Llandudno; it is now known as the Links Hotel.

THE SARAH NICOL MEMORIAL COTTAGE HOSPITAL

The Sarah Nicol Memorial Hospital, situated in Trinity Avenue, was opened in 1885. Sarah Nicol was the wife of Dr. James Nicol, the town Medical Officer and author of *The Climate of Llandudno*. Among the more interesting patients treated here were two Red Indians who were with a travelling circus. The building is now occupied by the Youth Centre.

LLANDUDNO AND DISTRICT HOSPITAL

The new Llandudno and District hospital, replacing the Sarah Nicol Memorial Hospital in Trinity Avenue, was opened on 12th August 1939 by H.R.H. Princess Alice, grand-daughter of Queen Victoria. (Artist's impression drawn by J. Hankers).

THE RAILWAY CONVALESCENT HOME, LLANDUDNO, FRONT VIEW

THE RAILWAY CONVALESCENT HOME

Situated below the Marine Drive on land which sites the Bishops Palace or Gogarth Abbey, it was purchased in 1894 by Mr. W.F. Mason who built the imposing building as his home. The land and building were purchased by the Railway Convalescent homes in 1949 and opened 9th May, 1950.

1. Llandudno. Lady Forester's Convalescent Home.

LADY FORESTER'S CONVALESCENT HOME

Following a generous bequest of £500,000 from Lady Forester, the convalescent home was built in conjunction with Much Wenlock Hospital in Shropshire. When the home opened in 1904, it accommodated 60 convalescent patients from the hospital and from within a certain defined area of Shropshire.

LLANDUDNO FROM DEGANWY, c. 1902

An early view of the town showing the 1899 gasometer and, alongside the 150 ft-high chimney part of the combined refuse incinerator and steam turbine generator. The smaller chimney nearby was associated with the Llandudno Brick, Lime and Stone Company.

THE GOLF LINKS, c. 1905

The North Wales Golf Club opened as a nine-hole course in 1894, extended later that year to 18 holes. The Maesdu Links opened in 1915. The white building, centre right is Maesdu Farm.